# Starting an
# eBay® Business

## SOCRATES™
**KNOW HOW TO DO MORE
AND SAVE**

Socrates Media, LLC
227 West Monroe, Suite 500
Chicago, Illinois 60606

1.800.SOCRATES

www.socrates.com

Register your purchase at Socrates.com to receive free useful home and business tips.

Your registration code is located on the CD included with this book.

# Table of Contents

# Introduction

Across the country, and even beyond, intelligent, savvy sellers are using eBay® to market their items. In fact, in 2004, eBay reported 114 million registered users—and the number keeps climbing. With eBay shoppers in 28 countries, eBay reports these users are spending $1,000 per second on eBay, which totals $32 billion a year. Plus, in 2004, sellers posted 332 million listings.

eBay estimates that 430,000 people use the auction site as a full-time or part-time job, although the exact number is difficult to determine. It is also estimated that 80 percent of small businesses that have five or fewer employees use eBay to sell their merchandise. In less than a decade, eBay has become the No. 1 e-commerce site in 16 countries.

For the motivated entrepreneur, eBay spells opportunity. And, because eBay is still a "young" organization, this business forum should grow exponentially and provide ample opportunities for smart sellers. Also, because seller fees amount to only 7 percent of total sales, you can operate a store with minimal overhead.

This book will help you learn how to turn your buying and selling experience on eBay into a lucrative career, with strategies and tools that can help you be more profitable.

**Did You Know**

- there are approximately 22.9 million small businesses in the U.S.?
- there are an estimated 550,100 new employer businesses—a 0.9 percent increase over the previous year?
- small businesses hire a larger proportion of employees who are younger, older and part-time workers?—and small businesses:
    - provide approximately 75 percent of the net new jobs added to the economy
    - represent 99.7 percent of all employers
    - employ 50.1 percent of the private work force
    - provide 40.9 percent of private sales in the country
    - accounted for 39.1 percent of jobs in high technology sectors in 2001
    - accounted for 52 percent of private sector output in 1999
    - represent 97 percent of all U.S. exporters

# Chapter 1
# Is an eBay® Business Right for You?

There is no denying that starting a new business (or even maintaining an established one) is as difficult as it is rewarding. Keep this in mind: You will probably exhaust all your time and finances just to get your business rolling and then have to wait for your investment to pay off. Most companies do not break even until the sixth month—at the very earliest. Before you feast on any of the profits, you must pay all the bills, from rent to inventory materials to insurance and utilities. Along with all the rags-to-riches success stories you have heard are overwhelming failure rates. Eighty percent of new companies will not last 5 years, while one-third will not survive even the first year. Being your own boss is a risk you must be well prepared to take.

Blind ambition lures hoards of people into businesses they know nothing about. You should be drawn not by your dream, but by your clear vision, distinct knowledge and broad experience. No matter what sort of business you want to start, you need to investigate all aspects of the business before committing your time and finances to it. It is best to begin on a part-time basis in order to more accurately gauge your future success. Two-thirds of all new businesses begin as part-time pursuits.

Even with this daunting picture in mind, maybe you have successfully dabbled in buying and selling merchandise online. Maybe a few great sales whet your appetite for bigger returns. Maybe you are simply ready for a new career. Whatever factors are driving your interest in operating an eBay business, there are many issues that require careful consideration before you quit your day job. Make sure your enthusiasm and confidence is justified.

The best way to assure yourself that you are making the right move is to spend at least 6 months using eBay to buy and sell at least several items per week. Throughout this process, you will become familiar with eBay's rules and strategies, gain insight into which products sell, learn how to best present your merchandise and develop winning strategies.

## Necessary Skills

During this period, it is also important to be aware and recognize your strengths and weaknesses in terms of starting your own business. Here are some qualities and skills you should have:

- **Technological know-how.** Are you comfortable and competent with technology? Can you efficiently access and navigate the Internet? Can you resolve computer problems when they occur? Since a computer, Internet access and digital camera are essential to an eBay business, it is critical that you are able to properly maintain your equipment.

- **An eye for products others want.** Do you have an eye for the types of products others consider valuable? Do most of your postings sell? Are you tuned in to trends? Are you able to spot hot items because of your expertise?

- **Good communication skills.** Do you have good writing and communication skills to write and design postings that motivate buyers to buy? Since eBay is about motivating buyers with written words and product photos, good grammar and writing skills are important.

- **Exceptional selling and negotiating skills.** As a successful eBay entrepreneur, you may need to negotiate discounted prices for your inventory and also sell buyers on the value of your products.

- **Ability to remain focused and self-motivated.** Anyone who works from home knows that it is easy to be distracted by television, friends, children and chores, but success takes commitment to spending a significant portion of your day developing your business.

- **Supportive family and friends.** You will need to be sensitive to your family and friends' attitudes about your commitment. Family and friends can either be extremely supportive or not.

- **Knack for handling the ups and downs.** If you eventually quit your day job, you need to be comfortable with irregular earnings and no company benefits. However, being your own boss has its own rewards. You also need to maintain a positive attitude when an item does not sell or the winning bid is low.

If you identify with the above traits and enjoy the eBay experience, you probably have the right attitude and personality to be successful at managing your own eBay business.

| Tip |
| --- |
| To be a career eBay seller, you need to list at least 100 items each week. |

## Financial Considerations

If you are an experienced eBay seller, you should already have most of the tools you need to launch a business, which minimizes the need for investment capital, but most eBay sellers cannot immediately replace their paychecks with eBay sales.

Whether you are ready to quit your day job depends on your current income and how well your eBay efforts are paying off. Start by estimating how much income you will need to cover your current responsibilities. Do not forget to factor in your health insurance costs and other benefits that you will need to pay out-of-pocket. Also, include the state and federal income taxes you will need to pay. Divide your income total by 2,000, which represents the annual hours worked in most full-time jobs. The answer is your approximate hourly wage.

To find out how close you are to matching this income through eBay sales, estimate how much time you spend each month selling on eBay and divide that number by your average monthly sales minus your business expenses. It is important to accurately estimate your time and cost of doing business.

If your income and benefits total $48,000 each year, your hourly wage is $24. If you average 40 hours each month selling on eBay and your monthly total sales average $1,160, and the cost of products and expenses totaled $100, you are already matching your current income.

Other financial factors can allow you to start your eBay business sooner. You may have a spouse or family member who can cover financial obligations while you build your business. You may have savings that can support you. In addition, if you have little income, there is less at stake and more reason to make a full-time commitment to your new endeavor. Either way, building any business takes dedication and determination.

$$\frac{\text{Necessary Gross Annual Income + Benefits}}{2,000} = \text{Hourly Wage from Employment}$$

$$\frac{\text{Total eBay Sales - Related Expenses}}{\text{Hours Spent Selling on eBay}} = \text{Hourly Wage from Your eBay Business}$$

### Ballparking Your Income

When these two hourly wages match, you can seriously consider working on your eBay business full-time.

## Space Factors

While many people squeeze into a corner of the kitchen or bedroom to work on their computers, this arrangement will not support your eBay success. To operate your business, you will need more space. An extra bedroom is ideal, but you may also have sufficient space in your basement, attic or large closet—anywhere that can accommodate your computer equipment, filing cabinet and staging area for taking photos of your merchandise. Most importantly, you must make the commitment to use your time wisely to address and efficiently manage the considerations listed above.

| Benefits | Challenges |
| --- | --- |
| Convenience of working from home | Replacing and managing steady income |
| Greater income potential | Acquiring marketable goods |
| Connect in one of the world's largest marketplaces | Being consistently disciplined |
| Pride in owning your own business | Learning how to comply with local, state and federal business laws |
| Opportunity to learn about diverse merchandise in a diverse marketplace | Becoming familiar with eBay's rules and strategies |

**Two Rules to Remember**

Most businesses fail because they fall short of unrealistic expectations. Planning for the worst will prepare you for the best. Remember these two simple but insightful adages known as Sheldon's Laws:

1. Things take three times as long as predicted. Bureaucracy, paperwork and other priorities inevitably delay even the most conservative deadlines.

2. Things cost twice as much as predicted. Maintenance fees, telephone bills, office supplies, marketing expenses, and collection costs typically add up well beyond meticulously calculated budgets.

# Chapter 2
# Getting Started

When you sell an item at your garage sale, you are not operating as an ongoing business, so many small business laws do not apply to these transactions. However, when you plan on making a living selling various items, you must be sure to operate according to the law like any other small business owner. This requires deciding how your business is structured, investigating necessary licenses, and complying with other local, state and federal regulations.

## Establishing Your Business with eBay

If you are new to eBay, you will have to register as a member first—then establish your sellers account. If you are not familiar with eBay, it is wise to learn more before becoming a seller. Buying will teach you about eBay from the customer's perspective and help you become familiar with the rules and jargon. This is also a valuable way to learn to recognize items and different sales tactics, see about potential prices and shipping costs and become familiar with payment methods. You may even get ideas about merchandise you had never considered selling.

1. **Register as a Member and Create Your Identity.**
   eBay's registration page will ask for your name and contact information. Carefully consider your user name. Do not use your real name, actual e-mail address or other identifiers. If you choose a name that has already been taken, eBay will provide you with options. Then choose a unique password in order to heighten the security of your financial and personal information. The next step is to review

the User Agreement. Completing the registration process initiates a confirmation e-mail to you, which you need to respond to in order to become official. This step also automatically registers you for eBay's sister site, Half.com, which you will learn about later in this book.

### Tip

When you log into eBay's home page, you can request to be logged in automatically, but it will only work from your computer.

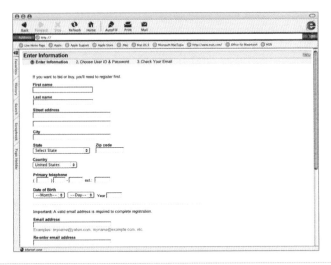

eBay's Registration Page

**2. Create a Seller's Account.**
The next step is to establish a seller's account. This step validates your user ID and password. To sell an item you need to provide your credit card and checking account information. This step allows eBay to verify that you are of legal age, identifiable to the specified financial institution and serious about selling.

This information is protected, encrypted and secure, so you can feel confident your information will not be available to others.

## More about You

eBay offers an area on their site called About You that you can use to provide information to your customers. Although this page is optional, it may be helpful to sellers to know a little bit about you, especially if you are experienced in a particular area related to your products.

To locate this page, go to the site map and click on the About Me link. Follow the prompts and you will find a page where you can fill in a title, welcome message, introduction paragraph and upload a photo. Write your listing in a word processing program that will check your spelling and grammar. Then cut and paste the information into this page. When you share your intention to provide your buyers with great products and service, you will build trust that will inspire confidence in your buyers—and help generate repeat customers.

### eBay's Auction Management Software

Fortunately, eBay has created several auction management tools to assist you in listing your items. Turbo Lister and Seller's Assistant offer eBay sellers functions that can save time.

eBay's Turbo Lister

### eBay's Turbo Lister

One way to quickly list your items is to download eBay's free Turbo Lister, easily accessed through eBay's site map. You can download the program to your PC (Macintosh computers are currently not supported) and enter your items offline at your leisure. Here is how Turbo Lister can help:

- Up to 3,000 items can be uploaded in a single effort.
- Using the template can enhance your listings or you can create your own.

- Active or completed listings can also be imported to Turbo Lister.
- Auctions can take place immediately or scheduled for peak bidding times.
- Calculate your listing fees—you can make adjustments if your fees are too high.

### eBay's Seller's Assistant

To help manage the selling process, eBay also provides Selling Manager and Selling Manager Pro, which can help medium to high volume sellers more efficiently manage sales. Although eBay charges a small monthly fee for these tools, the expense could be well worth it. Both can help:

- access your sales online, straight from the My eBay selling tab
- monitor your active listings in real time
- track buyer e-mails, bulk sold and unsold items
- track which buyers have paid and left feedback
- print invoices and shipping labels
- buyers combine payments for multiple items

**Tip**

Visit eBay's site map to access answers to questions you may have.

## Establishing Your Business Office

Even though you may have a home office for casual eBay selling, you will find that managing a home-based business requires even more space. Ideally, you need a separate room where you can set up an office. If you will be selling large items or quantities, you may also need additional space to store your inventory.

### Supplies and Equipment

Your most important piece of equipment is your computer. If you have been using eBay with an outdated computer, this is the right time to replace it with one that has sufficient memory and a fast processor. You should have a PC with at least 60GB of storage and at least 512MB RAM with a CD-RW drive. If you have been using dial-up services, you should also consider a DSL or cable line for high-speed access. You can waste considerable time waiting for information to come up on your screen—and time is money!

Important communication tools include: a dedicated telephone line, economical long distance service to resolve customer's issues, and fax capabilities, which may be included in your computer.

## Software

As a business owner, it is critical that you keep accurate financial records, so work with an accountant to set up accounts that will help you manage assets, inventory, orders and returns. You will also need a spreadsheet program to track inventory, a word processing program to create ads and a photo management program to help you crop and edit merchandise photos.

Most importantly, invest in virus protection software and make sure you run it regularly. You will need to periodically back up your data to a CD or auxiliary hard drive. Constant Internet activity makes your computer vulnerable to a variety of viruses that can destroy files and damage your computer.

## Tools to Monitor Operations

If you do not use eBay's auction management software or you use multiple auction sites, you will need to set up files that will track total sales, chart your progress and help keep you organized. Even if you use the auction management software, it is a good idea to create your own log with fields that display more comprehensive sales activity information. This will require developing several spreadsheet documents and keeping them up-to-date.

## Expense Tracking

For tax purposes, as well as measuring your success, you need a spreadsheet that tracks your expenses. Any spreadsheet program should be sufficient. Your expenses should include:

- capital expenses, which are mostly one-time expenses, such as your computer, camera, software, fax machine, office furniture and copier
- home office costs (regular and exclusive expenses based on a percentage of the space in your home that is used to operate your business, e.g., rent, mortgage, mortgage interest and utilities)
- fees for legal and accounting assistance
- phone expenses
- Internet provider costs

- auction management software fees
- listing fees (break down special feature fees so you can see if they are worthwhile for your merchandise)
- the gas or travel expenses you pay to visit sources to shop for inventory
- the cost of your merchandise
- postage and shipping costs to acquire or sell your merchandise
- shipping supplies
- storage costs

To be sure you are not forgetting anything, ask your accountant about which expenses should be logged and how to enter them in the software you have selected.

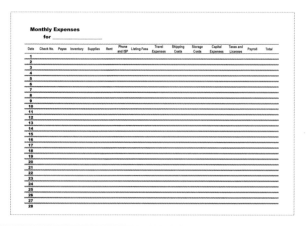

Track your expenses with this form.

### Inventory Database

Your spreadsheet program can also help you manage your inventory. Set up a document so you can have an up-to-date list of all your items with relevant information. Over time, this document can help you compare prices from different sources and report inventory purchases for tax purposes. Label the fields to include:

- date acquired
- item
- description

- purchase price
- source's name/contact
- notes

**Inventory**

| Date Acquired | Item | Descripton | Purchase Price | Source | Source Contact | Notes |
|---|---|---|---|---|---|---|

Keep track of your inventory with this form.

## Sales Tracking

Your spreadsheet program will come in handy in tracking sales as well. Set up a document so you can have an up-to-date list of all your items. You can also use this document to gauge what items are most profitable. Label the fields to include:

- eBay item number
- item
- listing/insertion fee
- special feature fees
- start date
- end date
- final price
- payment type
- buyer's contact information
- date shipped
- shipper
- tracking number
- shipping costs

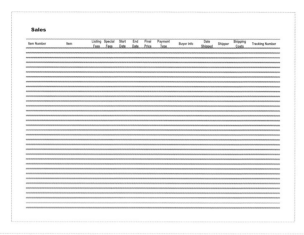

Keep track of sales with this form.

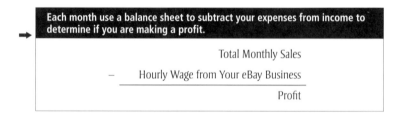

**Each month use a balance sheet to subtract your expenses from income to determine if you are making a profit.**

Total Monthly Sales

−  Hourly Wage from Your eBay Business

Profit

## Managing Your Time

Are your shopping excursions yielding great finds that are increasing your sales? Is time spent crafting a dynamic ad moving your items more quickly? Create a time tracker and find out. With a little analysis–by comparing where you place your efforts to your monthly sales–you may use your time tracker to gauge which tasks are most beneficial to your business. You might also find that you are putting more time into a particular task than is actually profitable. Your time tracker can also be useful in examining where additional help is needed when you are ready to expand.

Additionally, if you are new to self-employment, it is easy to get distracted and find a week has floated by without having accomplished much. Your time tracker can help keep you more disciplined. Include these fields:

- research
- purchasing

- creating listings
- photography
- posting listings
- customer service
- personal time

At the end of each day, record your time. Then revisit your time tracker at the end of the week and make sure you have spent approximately 40 hours on tasks that directly generate business.

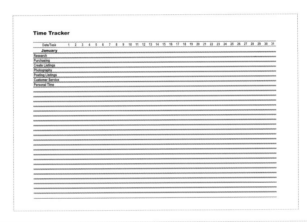

Manage your time with this form.

### Time Is Money

In the beginning, you may find that balancing the time you spend buying items to sell and managing your sales is awkward. You also do not want to buy so much that you have storage issues, but you do not want to run out of merchandise to sell. You always want to have items on auction. If you are buying in bulk, you will need to put more energy into the sales tasks. If your merchandise tends to be one-of-a-kind, hunting it down might require more time. This means your items should be of higher value, because you will need to get a higher price to pay for your time. Either way, it may take you a few months to get a feel for how much time to put into each task to be most profitable—which is why keeping an accurate timesheet is important!

## Establish Payment Options

You should already have a good idea of payment options, but as a business, you may want to revisit which options will work best for you. Plus, as a business, more options will be open to you. Keep in mind that the more options you offer buyers, the easier it will be for them to buy.

If your *PayPal account is tied to your personal checking account, and you have created a business account, you should revise your preferences so money is deposited in your business account.

*PayPal is now owned by eBay.

| Payment Method | Advantages | Disadvantages |
|---|---|---|
| PayPal, PayDirect and other online payment systems | • Convenient<br>• Both parties assured of getting money/item | • Must be comfortable with sharing financial information with online service<br>• Must set up account in advance |
| Credit Cards | • May be most convenient for buyer | • Must set up merchant credit card account through a bank<br>• You need good credit to do this, and you will pay a small fee for every transaction |
| Personal Checks | • Some buyers may prefer this method<br>• Some may use only this method | • Check could bounce—wait until the check clears before you ship the item<br>• It can take 7-10 days for a check to clear |
| Money Orders | • Convenient to buyers who do not have credit cards or prefer not to share financial information<br>• A bank will deposit a money order immediately | • Easy to counterfeit—wait for your bank to accept it before you ship the item |
| COD (Cash on Delivery) | • None for the seller | • Dangerous—seller can be left with no payment and no back up from online auction, |
| Online Escrow Service: Will hold payment until buyer confirms item arrived safely, then forwards the payment to the seller. If there is a dispute, the escrow service may be willing to act as a referee. Allows credit card payments and insures shipment. | • The utmost security for both parties<br>• Ideal for high-priced items | • Services usually charge a 5 percent fee—typically paid by the buyer<br>• May add considerable time to transaction<br>• Beware of phony online escrow services |

# Chapter 3
# Learn about Buying

Now that you are an eBay member, you will want to experience eBay from a buyer's perspective—in any business, it is important to understand your customers.

## About Categories

Begin by browsing eBay's categories of goods, which range from dolls to DVDs. Each major category contains a variety of subcategories.

The subcategories allow you to go beyond a title search and onto the descriptions. At the top of the page, there is an advanced search function. Using this tool, you can search by keyword, item number, in specific category or throughout the site. Browsing and searching will show you how important it is to craft a title that will come up in buyers' searches.

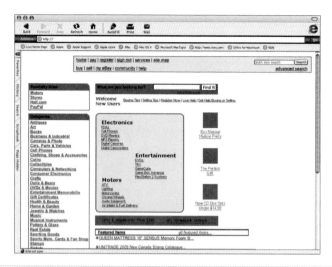

Example of eBay's categories

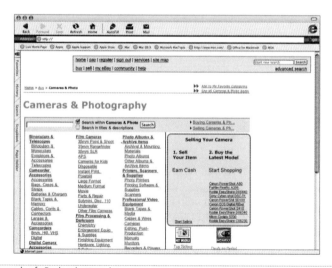

Example of eBay's subcategories

Clicking on more search options allows you to locate items by:

- ending date of auction
- minimum and maximum price
- specific sellers
- specific locations
- type of currency
- items in lots/multiple item listings
- Buy it Now items
- proximity to your zip code

The following guide lists popular terms and acronyms sellers use so buyers locate items easily.

| Guide to Acronyms | | | |
|---|---|---|---|
| BIN | Buy It Now | NBW | Never Been Worn |
| FS | Factory Sealed | NIB | New in Box |
| GU | Gently Used | NR | No Reserve |
| GW | Gently Worn | NWT | New with Tags |
| MWT | Mint with Tags | S/H | Shipping & Handling |

## Placing Your Bid

Once you locate the item you want to purchase, you may have two options. Some sellers offer buyers a Buy it Now option that lets the buyer immediately purchase the item at a posted price—or place a bid.

You will also notice that buyers often wait until an auction is nearly finished in order to place their bids, which means an item that began at 99 cents gathers a great deal of interest toward the end. The final bid can even exceed the usual retail price. Keep this in mind when you post your items. A low beginning price can attract interest. However, you need to be careful that you make a profit, so consider adding the Buy It Now feature.

You will also notice that some sellers include a reserve price. This price is the lowest price the seller is willing to take for the item. It is more appropriate for expensive items that need to recoup costs.

As a buyer, you should also review the seller's feedback, acceptable payment methods and shipping options. Feedback from other buyers will tip you off to a seller that is marketing products that may not reflect the quality you expect or delivering items too slowly. Whatever the case, feedback will provide some insight into what you might expect from this seller.

It is also important to check to make sure you can accommodate the seller's payment method. PayPal is a popular way to pay for auction merchandise, because it can transfer funds from your checking account to the seller's, without breaching your privacy. However, if you have not already visited the PayPal Web site to set up an account (www.paypal.com), it can take a few days to verify the process. That is why it is important to set up your account before buying or selling—you do not want negative feedback reporting that you are slow to pay. Many larger sellers also accept credit cards, so there are a variety of options.

Shipping costs are another factor to consider. It is the buyer's responsibility to list the shipping method he/she is willing to consider, so it is possible that your shipping costs can exceed the value of your item. In some cases, this may not matter. Other times, you may find shipping costs make the item less of a bargain than you expected.

When you are ready to place your bid, note the increments bidders have used. eBay sets up bidding increments based on the opening and reserve bids.

During the auction, e-mail the seller with questions you may have regarding the product or about shipping. This is the right time to resolve any questions—before they inhibit a smooth transaction.

Check how many bids have been placed and how many buyers have placed those bids. You should be able to gauge if several buyers are determined to win the item with a bidding war. If so, and you are equally determined, you will need to check the item often, especially in the final hours and outbid them.

If you win the auction, you need to follow through with payment, according to the seller's terms. This is an opportunity to use your PayPal account or an alternative method. Depending on the shipping, your item should arrive on your doorstop and complete the transaction.

**Consider Proxy Bidding**

Found a great item, but cannot sit at your computer outbidding other buyers? eBay has an automatic bidding system that allows you to enter the maximum amount you are willing to pay for an item. The system will place bids on your behalf according to eBay's increment schedule until you have won the item or another buyer outbids you.

## Provide Feedback

Once you safely receive your purchase, it is important to provide feedback. Your report lets other buyer's know what to expect and gives the seller an opportunity to accommodate your needs or defend his/her reputation. Feel free to comment on:

- ease of transaction
- prompt delivery
- accurate description
- condition of item upon arrival

The seller may also give you positive feedback. This is your first opportunity to build a list of complementary exchanges that you can refer back to when you are doing the selling. Positive feedback, on either side of the transaction is a wonderful way to build repeat customers.

**eBay as a Source**

Do not overlook buying on eBay as a source for your merchandise. By winning an undervalued item in an auction, you may be able to resell it to a local vendor or even re-list it on eBay.

# Chapter 4
# Build Your Inventory

Evolving your eBay hobby into a career means selling at a higher volume. You need to explore many sources for items to sell. Even if you already have an idea of the items you are most comfortable selling, look into identifying multiple vendors.

## Line Up Sources

Most eBay sellers rely on several sources to maintain their inventory. Identifying appropriate sources depends on many factors. Ask these questions:

- How much of an investment can you make in one supplier's merchandise?
- Will the purchase incur shipping fees that can be recouped so you can retain your profits?
- Is the supplier reliable?
- Does the volume purchased require too much storage space?
- Is the vendor reliable?
- Can the vendor promptly fill orders and accommodate your payment plan?
- For better prices, can you wait to purchase the items off-season?

Here are a few types of sources you can use to find marketable items:

## Your Inner Circle

If casual eBay selling has not emptied out your closets, garage and attic, you may have enough merchandise to launch your business. There are several advantages to starting with your own goods. First, you will not have to invest money in purchasing inventory or additional storage space. Plus, since the merchandise is yours, you can vouch for its history and quality first-hand. You also know that since you were once willing to purchase it, someone else may be likely to purchase it as well.

When you have sorted through your own goods, you can ask friends and relatives to let you help them sell their goods. Many people would be happy to turn over their unused items for a fraction of the cost—and word-of-mouth can almost guarantee a continual flow of merchandise into your inventory. However, dealings with family members and friends can be tricky, so you need to set up a firm purchasing policy upfront for all your suppliers. Make sure you address these issues:

- Who pays to ship the item to you?

- Are you purchasing the item outright or on consignment?

- If purchasing on consignment, what percentage of the sales price will your "supplier" receive?

Be sure the agreed upon percentage will reward you for your time as well as any associated acquisition/shipping costs. The disadvantage to relying on your inner circle is the limited merchandise.

### Tip

Check out eBay's Hot Categories Report for insight into what merchandise is currently moving the fastest.

## Acquiring Merchandise

Garage sales, flea markets and thrift stores offer excellent opportunities to find auctionable items. People who frequent these sources for the sole purpose of re-selling are called "pickers." Since these purchases are likely to be one-of-a-kind, you are better off using these sources to track down items in your area of expertise.

If you want to sell high volumes of lower-priced goods, dollar stores can offer some opportunities to acquire inventory. If you are confident that a particular item would generate sales, talk to the store manager about purchasing a higher quantity at a reduced price.

Dollar store purchasing agents and closeout vendors buy liquidated, overstock and returned merchandise from large retailers, wholesalers and government entities at a fraction of the cost. You can also arrange to purchase overstocks from a favorite local retailer or buy bulk items from a closeout company.

**Visit These Closeout Sources:**

American Merchandise Liquidators: www.amlinc.com

Closeout.com: www.closeout.com

closeoutnow.com: www.closeoutnow.com

Closeout Specialists: www.closeouts.digiscape.net

Liquidation.com: www.liquidation.com

Overstock.com: www.overstockb2b.com

GB Retail Exchange: www.retailexchange.com

WholesaleCentral.com: www.wholesalecentral.com

## Artists and Craftspeople

Many creative people prefer putting their energy into creating a beautiful object rather than marketing it—which creates an opportunity for you. A beautifully designed piece of jewelry or hand-carved bowl can be very desirable to many eBay shoppers. Plus, because the artist usually has low overhead, you should be able to sell the piece at a price for an amount that will be profitable for both of you.

To buy items outright, attend arts and crafts fairs. A Google™ or Yahoo® search of arts and crafts, plus your location, should yield announcements of fairs that are convenient for you to attend. For more locations, you can also visit www.artandcraftshows.net.

Because fine art is unique and more expensive, selling it profitably is more challenging. In this case, you should take the item on consignment and negotiate a commission with the artist.

## Trade Shows

Once you have your sales tax number, you can gain access to most trade shows. Here, you will be able to buy a variety of goods at a great price from a number of sources. Vendors will supply ample information on their products and be open to creating an ongoing mutually beneficial relationship. If you are considering attending trade shows, shop regional and national shows where wholesalers are more prominent.

When you attend a trade show, be businesslike and do not hesitate to tell vendors you are starting an eBay business. Be generous in distributing your business card and do not hesitate to push for a great deal.

**To Locate Appropriate Trade Shows Visit:**

Trade Show Plaza: www.tradeshowplaza.com

Tradeshow Week: www.tradeshowweek.com

TSNN: www.tsnn.com

## What to Buy

Even if you already know what type of merchandise you want to list, it is a good idea to understand which products sell more quickly. According to eBay, products move with the speed shown in the chart.

| Products | Number Sold on eBay Per Hour |
|---|---|
| Toys | 154,800 |
| Small kitchen appliances | 60 |
| Cell phones | 102 |
| Cell phone chargers | 41 |
| PDAs | 44 |
| MP3 players | 38 |
| Video games | 833 |
| Diamond rings | 30 |
| Books | 3,600 |
| Digital cameras | 120 |
| Desktop computers | 34 |
| Music CDs | 780 |

## What NOT to Buy–Prohibited and Restricted Items

While you have an eye out for marketable merchandise, keep in mind that eBay prohibits or restricts some items from being sold through their site. You can visit http://pages.ebay.com/help/policies/items-ov.html for information and rules concerning:

Academic Software

Airline and Transit Related Items

Alcohol (Also See Wine)

Animals and Wildlife Products

Anti-Circumvention Policy

Artifacts

Authenticity Disclaimers

Autographed Items

Batteries

Beta Software

Bootleg Recordings

Brand Name Misuse

Catalog Sales

Catalytic Converters and Test Pipes

Charity or Fundraising Listings

Comparison Policy

Compilation and Informational Media

Contracts and Tickets

Counterfeit Currency and Stamps

Counterfeit Items

Credit Cards

Downloadable Media

Drugs and Drug Paraphernalia

Electronics Equipment

Embargoed Goods and Prohibited Countries

Encouraging Infringement

Policy

Event Tickets

Faces, Names and Signatures

Firearms, Ammunition, Replicas and Militaria

Fireworks

Food

Freon and Other Refrigerants

Gift Cards

Government IDs and Licenses

Hazardous, Restricted and Perishable Items

Human Parts and Remains

Importation of Goods into the United States

International Trading-Buyers

International Trading-Sellers

Lockpicking Devices

Lottery Tickets

Mailing Lists and Personal Information

Manufacturers' Coupons

Mature Audiences

Medical Devices

Misleading Titles

Mod Chips, Game Enhancers and Boot Discs

Movie Prints

Multi-Level Marketing, Pyramid and Matrix Programs

OEM Software

Offensive Material

Pesticides

Plants and Seeds

Police-Related Items

Postage Meters

Pre-Sale Listings

Prescription Drugs and Devices

Promotional Items

Real Estate

Recalled Items

Recordable Media

Replica and Counterfeit Items

Satellite and Cable TV Descramblers

Slot Machines

Stocks and Other Securities

Stolen Property

Surveillance Equipment

Tobacco

Travel

Unauthorized Copies

Used Clothing

Warranties

Weapons and Knives

Wine (Also See Alcohol)

## Pricing Strategies

In the mid to late 1990s, eBay was a market ripe with unusual and quirky items for which people were willing to pay outrageous prices. Like any novelty, the thrill quickly faded, but savvy sellers can still make money selling a huge variety of goods. The trick is to identify the items that will bring you the most profit.

Pop-culture novelties still bring a good price. Antique furniture, tools or accessories can be very profitable, even when younger than the 100 years that define antiques. Vintage items, such as clothing or magazines that are only 20 or 30 years old, are also often highly prized. Packaging, whether from a cereal box or soup can is also valuable to many—but the item must be in pristine condition. Old newspapers, ads or promotional items, like fast-food giveaways, are prime eBay merchandise as well.

> **Tip**
>
> To help ensure profitability, try to acquire inventory that will provide at least a 75-150 percent return on investment.

### Compare Completed Listings

Whatever your particular merchandise is, you can gauge a price by checking out your item's sales potential and by searching in the Completed Listings from the sidebar. Browse eBay's auction archives to see final prices on items sold in the past 3 weeks. To get there, go to the Web site and run a search on the type of item you are selling. Once you are on any auction-listing page, click Completed Listings in the left navigation bar.

This will yield a list of items and their winning bids. If you specify that you want the search sorted by highest price first, you can see the potential. Study these listings for information on what qualities differentiate the merchandise. How much more does an item in good condition bring? What qualities add or subtract from the value? Are the items rare enough that buyers will pay more? How did the seller present the products to make them more desirable?

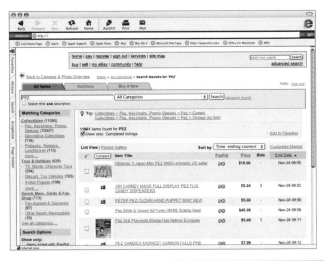

Compare winning bids with a search in "Completed listings."

## What Is It Really Worth?

No matter where you are posting your auction, the most important thing you must decide on is the minimum price you are willing to accept. How do you know how much an item is really worth? To find out, research what similar goods have sold for. Here are some additional resources you can use to set your price:

- Search various online auction sites to watch the price bidding for similar items.

- Check manufacturer Web sites for their list prices on new items. *Note: If you are selling new products, you will not get the list price.*

- Study industry magazines for the current worth of collectibles, antiques and more.

- Hire an appraiser for big-ticket items.

- Add up your own costs.

### Tip

If other sellers are offering many of the same items, hold back until your competition sells out—you are more likely to collect a higher price.

## Pricing Options

On eBay you have three options regarding your listed pricing. The Beginning Bid determines where the bidding starts. You can start low, with 99 cents, to draw in bargain hunters, or be more realistic. It is up to you. Keep in mind that some eBay fees are based on your opening bid, so a low beginning bid of $1.00 will cost you the same as a beginning bid of $9.99. (Check the Insertion Fee Table on page 53 to see how your beginning bid will affect your listing fee.)

For a small fee, you can also opt to set a Reserve Price, which is refunded if your item sells. This is the lowest bid you will accept. If your reserve price is not met, you can decline to sell the item. You do not have to fill in the reserve price, and your reserve price is not disclosed to bidders. Buyers will be told that your item has a reserve price and whether that price has been met. If you do not use a reserve price, you must sell the item to the highest bidder.

### Fees for Setting a Reserve Price are as Follows:

| Reserve Price | Reserve Price Auction Fee |
|---|---|
| $ .01 to $49.99 | $1.00 |
| $50.00 to $199.99 | $2.00 |
| $200.00 and up | 1% of the Reserve Price or maximum fee of $100 |

If you are selling a motor vehicle, there is a $2.00 maximum reserve fee. Plus, reserve price listings are not available for multiple item listings (Dutch Auctions).

Or you can set a fixed price, called Buy It Now. This feature allows you to specify the price you will accept for your item. The first buyer who accepts your price wins the item.

With Buy It Now, you eliminate bidding wars and setting a reserve price. You post the price you want and a lucky buyer can purchase it immediately. However, you must meet one of these requirements before being allowed to use Buy It Now:

• achieve at least "10" as a feedback score

• contact information is verified using the ID Verify service

• have a PayPal account, achieve a feedback score of "5" and accept PayPal as a payment method

During the auction, if your buyer chooses to Buy It Now before the first bid comes in, your item sells immediately, and your listing is complete.

When a bid is offered first, the Buy It Now option disappears. In that case, the item listing proceeds as a normal auction. When you set a minimum, or Reserve Price, the Buy It Now feature disappears when the first bid reaches the Reserve Price.

**Tip**

Whether you choose a Buy It Now, Reserve Price or simply set a beginning bid, pay attention to how your choice can affect your eBay fee.

Only experience can tell you where to set your beginning bid, and whether to use a reserve price or Buy it Now. Different auction experts have differing opinions on these pricing matters.

**These Factors Drive Up Prices:**

- limited supply
- completeness
- excellent condition
- in-season or timeliness
- presentation

Also, consider the value of the product. If you found an item for 50 cents, such as a child's toy at a garage sale, you can afford to sell it for less than the merchant who purchased it through a wholesaler. Also, keep in mind that if you are spending money on digital photos, shipping and auction site fees, you need to make sure you are not losing money on your sale.

# Chapter 5
# List Your Items

Whether or not you are using Turbo Lister, make sure your listings are as effective as possible. This means choosing the appropriate selling format and category, writing an appealing description and a title that gets hits, and taking photos to quickly deliver accurate pictures to your potential buyers. Finally, you need to specify your price, learn your fees and factor in shipping.

The first step in listing your item is to click Sell on the home page. If you have not logged in, you will be asked to do so. Then, select a selling format. This sets up the type of sale you want. You can choose one of the following options:

- Online Auction
- Fixed Price
- Real Estate

When you choose your selling format, click Continue at the bottom of the screen.

Choosing your selling format

## Create Dynamic Listings

There are four important elements to your listing:

1. category
2. title
3. description
4. photo

Take time to write your listing in a word processing program. This will allow you to perform a spelling and grammar check. When you are satisfied with the content, you can copy and paste the listing into the online auction form.

### Category

Start by selecting the category where you will list your item. Be thorough when you research these. eBay provides a tool to help guide you through this step—you want your item to appear in as many searches as possible.

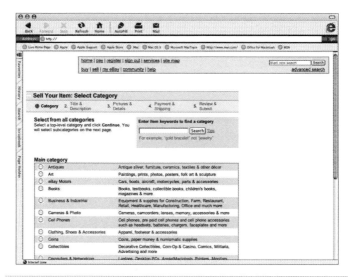

Select a category that best describes your item.

Next, you will be prompted to select a sub-category that is even more specific to your item. You can also select a second category, so that your listing will come up more often in searches. Adding a category, however, greatly increases your insertion and listing upgrade fees, so be careful.

## Title

Your title, or headline, is the most frequently read part of any sales letter or advertisement, and this is where you need to spend most of your time. This is your first chance to promote your item.

Your title can be up to 55 characters, so be concise, but complete and descriptive. Include specifics on brand name, make/model/year, etc. Bidders will search for these terms, so be accurate. *Note: eBay does not allow HTML enhancements in titles.*

### Tips for Better Titles

- Announce your sale with descriptive keywords.
- Include brand name, artist or designer.
- Tell buyers what your item is even if the category defines it.
- Use terms and words buyers might use in their searches.
- Avoid words like "wow" and "must have"—buyers do not necessarily search using these words.
- Get ideas from past listings of similar items that succeeded in winning high prices.

## Write a Description That Motivates Buyers

Your description is your most powerful selling tool. If you are going to make a success of your business, you must learn how to use words effectively. In addition, if your message is going to be successful, you need to manipulate the readers' emotions.

Choose your title and type your description.

### Tip

Misspellings and typos will eliminate words from showing up in a search and jeopardize your professional image, so proofread carefully!

The art and science of using words to earn sales is often referred to as copywriting. (Several books are written on this subject and noted in Appendix 1.) The first thing you should understand about copywriting is that you are trying to control your readers through their emotions, long enough to move them to action and bid on your items.

For the eBay seller, this means it is often worth telling a story behind your item or introducing emotional benefits. For instance, if you are selling a vase, telling your readers about the elderly woman who received the vase on her 25th wedding anniversary can be as important as stating the item's dimensions and material. If you are selling a comforter, you might add language that suggests that it is the perfect comforter for a cozy winter weekend.

**Tip**

People make decisions based on emotions, not logic.

### Lead with Benefits, Follow with Features

The old copywriting adage says, "lead with benefits, follow with features." A feature is a fact about your item. Specifics like size, color and material are all features.

The advantage the customer enjoys as a result of those features is benefit. One simple way to convert features to benefits is to ask yourself, "What is the advantage this feature gives my customer?" For example, a large size comforter may fit a larger variety of beds. A polyester blend fabric offers the convenience of being machine washable. The benefits usually hit the emotional side, and the features support those benefits.

**Tip**

Avoid using all capital letters in descriptions. Upper and lowercase letters are easier to read and do not cause online complaints.

### Be Creative

Try to use specific descriptive adjectives rather than "terrific" or "fantastic." Include the following in your description of each item:

- Keywords that bidders might use to search for your specific item
- Your e-mail address for questions (good customer service)
- Details on shipping/insurance/payment
- If appropriate, state where the item is from—estate sale, your grandmother's attic, etc.

After the description, add a paragraph on shipping/insurance/payment options, even though the information may be available elsewhere. Also, include your e-mail address for questions (good customer service) and, if you have expertise as an antiques dealer or a life-long comic book collector, say so.

Consider adding a statement such as "Your full payment will be refunded if you are not 100% satisfied with the condition of this item." It will reassure bidders that you are professional and honest.

Include any other terms or specifics. A thorough description, accompanied by clear, detailed terms of service, reassures bidders that you are professional and honest. When your description is complete, you may want to add HTML coding to enhance it. You can click on HTML Tips at the bottom of the description box for help.

**HTML Skills**

Many auction sites give you the opportunity to enhance your listing with basic HTML. You can learn to make portions of your text bold, italicize or colored and create large headlines—within a half hour. Visit these sites for tutorials on HTML:

www.htmlgoodies.com

www.htmlcodetutorial.com

www.trainingtools.com/online/html

hotwired.lycos.com/webmonkey/teachingtool/html.html

eBay offers layout tools that eliminate the need for HTML skills—but these cost extra.

### Be Honest

A good ad is about making the truth appealing. Be thorough and specific about the item's origin, condition, features, dimensions and other relevant details. Do not call something "one-of-a-kind" or "like new" if it is not. Use a model number if applicable or provide a link to the manufacturer's Web site for more detailed information on the item. You want to be as honest as possible, because a disappointed buyer may leave negative feedback, which can hurt future sales. Also, this field is virtually limitless, but be sensitive to how much information the shopper will want to read.

**Make Sure Your Listing Is:**

| | |
|---|---|
| • complete | • accurate |
| • easy to read | • able to inspire an emotional response |
| • error-free | |

## Enhancing Your Descriptions

Jazz up your listing with some lively descriptors. Here are a few to get you started:

| | | | |
|---|---|---|---|
| Absolutely | Funky | Novel | Sizable |
| Amazing | Genuine | Now | Special |
| Announcing | Gift | Odd | Startling |
| Approved | Gigantic | Only | Strange |
| Attractive | Glossy | Opulent | Strong |
| Authentic | Greatest | Original | Sturdy |
| Bargain | Guaranteed | Packaging | Successful |
| Beautiful | Hate | Outstanding | Superior |
| Better | Helpful | Personalized | Surprise |
| Big | Here | Playful | Terrific |
| Breakthrough | Highest | Popular | Tested |
| Charming | How | Powerful | Timeless |
| Colorful | How to | Practical | Treasure |
| Colossal | Huge | Pristine | Treasured |
| Complete | Immediately | Prized | Tremendous |
| Confidential | Improved | Professional | Unconditional |
| Coveted | Informative | Profitable | Unique |
| Crammed | Instructive | Profusely | Unlimited |
| Delivered | Interesting | Protect | Unparalleled |
| Direct | Largest | Proven | Unsurpassed |
| Discount | Latest | Quality | Untouched |
| Discover | Lavishly | Quickly | Unusual |
| Easily | Liberal | Rare | Useful |
| Elegant | Life | Reduced | Valuable |
| Endorsed | Lifetime | Refundable | Wealth |
| Enormous | Limited | Reliable | Weird |
| Excellent | Love | Remarkable | Well-Proportioned |
| Exciting | Lowest | Revealing | Whimsical |
| Exclusive | Lucky Find | Revolutionary | Windfall |
| Expert | Magic | Sale | Wonderful |
| Exquisite | Mammoth | Scarce | |
| Famous | Mint | Secrets | |
| Fascinating | Miracle | Security | |
| Fortune | Much-Loved | Selected | |
| Free | New | Sensational | |
| Full | Noted | Simplified | |

## Your Photos

A digital photo of your product is a critical element in your listing. Great photos require a little preparation, which will pay off in an auction. Find a spot where you can create your own photo studio. All it takes is a few feet of space, a table, a few options for backdrops, and good lighting and a camera. For eBay, you will need a digital photo—there are three ways you can create these:

1. Buy, rent or borrow a digital camera. A 2-megapixel camera promises good quality photos. You download the photos from the camera directly to your computer.

2. Scan your printed photos. You can purchase a flatbed scanner for $50 to $250—less expensive than a digital camera, but you still pay for film and developing. Once you Scan your traditional print photos, you have digital images.

3. Use a photo service. Take your roll of film—or your printed photos—wherever you usually have film developed. The vast majority of photo departments can now provide digital images on CD or over the Internet.

Place your item on a contrasting surface so it stands out. This means, if the item is dark, use a light surface and vice versa. Invest in a few yards of inexpensive fabric—solid white, off-white, navy or black will work best. A dark item on a dark background will absorb the item and not show up as well in your photo.

Stand close enough to capture the details. Use lighting to show detail. Natural light will produce the best results, but you can also use incandescent bulbs (60 watts or less). Aim the light where it is needed, but be sensitive to spots that might produce glare. When important, include another item in the shot to demonstrate size. For example, if you are selling earrings, place them in a hand so the viewer can more easily understand the correct size.

Take several photos that are tight close-ups, back views, side views and close-ups of notable features that might be of special interest to buyers. If you have photo-editing software, such as Adobe Photoshop®, you can crop, brighten and adjust your photos. Save your digital images as JPGs or GIFs. The files should be less than 30K to ensure your listing page loads quickly.

eBay allows all sellers to post one photo of their item. You can post more photos for 15 cents each. For an additional fee (75 cents to $1.50) you can post larger photos, a slide show or a picture pack, which shows up to a dozen views of your item. An intricate item with multiple sides, such as an ornate vase with carvings, could benefit from multiple views. However, you have to expect that additional photos will attract more interest and your winning bid should cover these extra charges.

## Complete Your Listing

Now you are ready to wrap up the listing process. After clicking on Continue at the bottom of the screen, you will be asked for:

- beginning bid and if desired, your reserve price;
- the duration of your auction;
- the date and time to start your auction (there is a 10 cents charge to delay starting it);
- the quantity of items in the listing—you can specify the number of items in a lot;
- item location–when selling large bulky items, you may specify pickup—sharing your location helps the buyer know how far he/she must travel to pickup the item;
- a photo of the item;
- your choice of visual themes–you can choose to frame your listing with one of dozens of graphic patterns or textures that can enhance your information;
- your choice of layout–most listings select the photo to the left of the copy;
- gallery options that offer additional opportunities to showcase your item–for example, for $19.95, a small version of your first picture(s) and listing can be showcased in the featured area of the Gallery;
- visual enhancements of your listing–for $1.00, your listing can be bold; for another $3.00 it can have a border—highlighting is $5.00—these treatments will make your listing stand out;
- special promotion services–if you have a feedback rating of 10+, you can purchase a Featured Plus! listing ($19.95) or placement on the home page ($39.95 for one item); ($79.95 for two items);
- gift services–this feature lets the buyers know that your item is appropriate for gift giving by adding a gift icon to your listing for 25 cents. If using this feature, you should include cost and details for supplying a gift card, gift wrap and express shipping; and
- page counter that announces your traffic volume.

As you can see, these special services can take a bite out of your profits, so use them wisely.

eBay gives you the information you need to efficiently set up your auction.

## Review Shipping Options

The final step in creating your listing is specifying payment and shipping information.

After clicking on Continue, you will be shown payment options. You should already have set up your PayPal account in order to accept credit card payments. You can also accept money orders or a cashier's check. Only sellers that have their own merchant Visa®, MasterCard®, Discover® or American Express® accounts can accept those payment methods.

Depending on what you are shipping, where you are located and your personal preferences, you will probably use one of the following services.

| Company | Pickup Options | Insurance/ Tracking | Convenient to You and Buyer |
|---------|----------------|---------------------|------------------------------|
| U.S. Postal Service® | Must drop off unless package is metered | No | Always |
| DHL® | Drop at drop box; will pickup at your home if you have an account | Yes | Possibly–depends on locations |
| FedEx® | Drop at drop box; will pick up at your home if you have an account | Yes | Probably |
| UPS® | Drop at drop box; will pickup at your home if you hold an account | Yes | Probably |

If you decide to go with the U.S. Postal Service® and will be selling a lot, consider buying or renting a postage meter machine. You pay for postage online and can apply metered stickers to packages. This allows you to drop smaller packages in mailboxes—packages without metered postage must be taken to a post office.

If you opt not to insure a package you ship, as the seller, you are responsible for reimbursement if the item is damaged en route.

### Tips

In each listing, specify that the buyer pays all shipping costs—but research the costs for shipping each item and include a specific dollar amount in your listing.

Factor your cost for boxes, envelopes, packing materials and other shipping costs and include this in your shipping information as "handling charge." Keep this as low as possible, because bidders are often sensitive about paying for this.

You must also specify where you are willing to ship and estimate shipping costs. This is your opportunity to limit shipments to foreign countries or local pickup—whichever is appropriate for your item. Remember, the more flexible you are, the more customers will be interested.

> **Tip**
>
> Pack fragile items in a box, then pack that box inside a larger box. Surround it with packing peanuts. A packaged item should be able to be dropped from five feet without breaking.

eBay offers a shipping calculator that will help you estimate this cost more accurately. Simply enter the weight and estimated size.

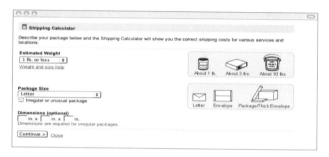

eBay's Shipping Calculator helps you estimate shipping costs.

Then, click on Continue and enter the possible destinations to get an estimate of what shipping should cost. The Shipping Calculator will display rates.

Enter destination to get an estimate of shipping cost.

## Keep Costs Down

You will find that eBay charges a variety of fees—from an Insertion Fee to enhancements to a Final Value Fee, once the sale is made. These fees can help move merchandise or eat away at your profits. Only experience will show you which enhancement helps you sell. Experiment. The first step however is to learn about the services and features that are available and how much they cost. Review the charts below.

> **Tip**
>
> If you cannot decide if your item should be priced at $9.99 or $10.00, you will save 25 cents by making your opening bid below $10.00.

## Insertion Fee

| Starting or Reserve Price | Insertion Fee |
|---|---|
| $ .01 - $0.99 | $0.30 |
| $1.00 - $9.99 | $0.35 |
| $10.00 - $24.99 | $0.60 |
| $25.00 - $49.99 | $1.20 |
| $50.00 - $199.99 | $2.40 |
| $200.00 - $499.99 | $3.60 |
| $500.00 or more | $4.80 |

## Final Value Fees

| Closing Price | Insertion Fee |
|---|---|
| Item not sold | No Fee |
| $0.01 - $25.00 | 5.25% of the closing value |
| $25.01 - $1,000.00 | 5.25% of the initial $25.00 ($1.31), plus 2.75% of the remaining closing value balance ($25.01 to $1,000.00) |
| Over $1,000.01 | 5.25% of the initial $25.00 ($1.31), plus 2.75% of the initial $25.00 - $1,000.00 ($26.81), plus 1.50% of the remaining closing value balance ($1,000.01 - closing value) |

The Insertion Fee for Multiple Item, Dutch Auction and Fixed Price Listings is based on the opening value of the items, which is the starting or the fixed item price multiplied by the quantity of your items. The maximum insertion fee for any Multiple Item Listing is $4.80.

## Reserve Price Fee

eBay also charges a fee if you choose to have a Reserve Price. This is the price that must be met before there is a sale. If the item sells, the Reserve Price Fee is refunded.

| Reserve Price | Fee |
|---|---|
| $ .01 to $49.99 | $1.00 |
| $50.00 - $199.99 | $2.00 |
| $200.00 or more | 1% or Reserve Price (up to $100.00) |

Listing Upgrade Fees

You can make your listing stand out, but use these upgrades sparingly. Although charges may seem small to add bold print or include a border, these features add up and detract from your profits.

## Listing Upgrade Fees

| Feature | Fee |
|---|---|
| Gallery | $0.25 |
| Listing Designer* | $0.10 |
| Item Subtitle | $0.50 |
| Bold | $1.00 |
| Buy It Now | $0.05 |
| Scheduled Listings | $0.10 |
| 10-Day Duration | $0.20 |
| Border | $3.00 |
| Highlight | $5.00 |
| Featured Plus! | $19.95 |
| Gallery Featured | $19.95 |
| Home Page Featured | $39.95 |
| Quantity of 2 or more | $79.95 |
| Gift Services | $0.25 |

*There is no listing fee for Selling Manager Pro subscribers.

The fees above are as of 1/1/2005 and change frequently

Visit http://pages.ebay.com/help/sell/fees.html before you finalize your listing for a complete list of fees and options. Then preview your listing and make any necessary corrections or changes. When you are finished, click on Submit. Your auction will be immediately active, but may not be found in search results until the search function is updated, which happens hourly. Until then, you can search for your item with your user

ID. eBay will also send you a confirmation e-mail message that your listing has been successfully submitted.

**Monitor Your Time**

Always remember that time is money. If your Time Tracker shows you have spent excessive time crafting your listing or trying to take the perfect photo, make an effort to speed up the process.

## Timing Is Everything

Auction experts believe that posting your listing at certain times, and the auction duration, can make a big difference. Determine how long you want your auction to last. Keep in mind that:

* eBay and other sites limit auctions to 3, 5, 7 or 10 days. Five or 7 days should be enough time for interested bidders to find and participate in the auction.

* The important factor is to plan when your auction will end. You want your auction to close at a time when you are available to watch the bidding and answer any questions via e-mail.

* Auction authorities agree that the prime time to end auctions is early afternoon or evening on a Sunday.

* Some experts point out that starting and ending on a Saturday afternoon or evening allows a 7-day auction to span two weekends, which might increase your exposure. Most bidders are home and at their computers on weekends.

Consider the four time zones across the United States and try to hit somewhere between 6:30 p.m and 8:30 p.m, Pacific Standard Time (PST).

# Chapter 6
# Manage Your Sales

You might think that once your listing is up and running, you can sit back and wait for the money. This will not work if you are going to build a business. Just as if you were running a retail store, between acquiring new merchandise or wrapping an item to ship, you need to be available to shoppers who need their questions promptly answered.

Take the opportunity to build your business by interacting with your buyers so that they leave great feedback about your service and your products. A positive experience can also motivate your buyers to look for you when they need your merchandise, or buy from you when your name appears on a search. A buyer can also put you on his/her list of favorite sellers.

**Tip**

The time to work on gaining a loyal customer is not after your item is sold, it is during the selling process.

### Get to Know a Variety of Personalities

When dealing with buyers, you will encounter a large variety of people. Some are savvy, easy-going and knowledgeable. Others are inexperienced, cautious and particular. Unfortunately, there are also the difficult and demanding shoppers. Learn to handle customers to your advantage.

### New Shoppers

There are plenty of people who have never participated in an online auction. Although eBay has made a commitment to building a user-friendly site, some new shoppers may be intimidated by the process. When you encounter a buyer who expresses lack of knowledge or simply asks questions that reveal inexperience, do not hesitate to help. Walk him or her through the process.

While some sellers may not provide this level of service, by meeting shoppers needs, you are setting yourself apart from the other sellers. While this may require a little extra effort, you will gain shoppers' loyalty and trust.

### Impatient Buyers

Some buyers want their merchandise instantly. Of course, how quickly they receive their package depends also on how fast they pay. It can help to acknowledge their concerns with e-mails that report when the payment arrives and when the item is shipped. Encouraging them to pay for a shipper who offers online tracking can transfer the burden of follow-up questions to the shipper.

### Cautious Buyers

In spite of secure Web sites and online banking, many customers still distrust online shopping. In this case, a professional style and communicating how the sale will take place can calm their fears. If they have reservations, you can suggest escrow, insurance and package tracking—all at their expense.

### Disgruntled Buyers

Some buyers will try to negotiate a lower price after winning the bid. They may even start to question the quality of the item in an attempt to get you to reduce the price. This practice is against auction rules. Stand your ground and if they remain obstinate, consider ending the deal and reporting them to eBay's SafeHarbor area as a nonpaying bidder.

**Tip**

eBay allows you to forego selling your item to the highest bidder if you sense a scammer. In such cases, you are free to sell your item to the next highest bidder.

## Nonpaying Customers

The eBay User Agreement and Unpaid Item Policy both specify that buyers must pay for the items they commit to purchase. To help, eBay provides an online process that facilitates communication between the buyer and seller to resolve the situation.

There are usually four steps to the Unpaid Item process:

### 1. File an unpaid item dispute

Report instances of an unpaid item up to 45 days from the date the buyer committed to buying and the seller committed to selling. Usually, to file an unpaid item dispute, the seller must wait 7 days after a listing closes. However, the following exceptions allow the seller to immediately file a dispute:

- at the time of the filing the buyer is no longer a registered user of eBay

- the buyer's country of origin is one in which the seller has indicated they will not ship

In either case, the buyer receives an unpaid item strike and the seller receives a Final Value Fee Credit.

### 2. eBay contacts the buyer

When the seller files an Unpaid Item Dispute, eBay notifies the buyer via e-mail. If the buyer signs it within 14 days of the filing he/she has an opportunity to respond. There are four subsequent paths the sale can take:

1. eBay sends a friendly reminder to pay. The message also contains simple instructions on how to respond or how to pay for the item. If the buyer does not pay within 7 days, the seller may file for a Final Value Fee Credit. The seller also becomes eligible to re-list the item for free.

2. A Mutual Agreement Note appears when the seller files the Unpaid Item Dispute, and reports that a mutual agreement has been reached with the buyer not to complete the transaction. Then eBay asks the buyer for confirmation via an e-mail and pop-up. When the buyer confirms the mutual agreement to abort the sale, the buyer does not receive an Unpaid Item Strike. Then the seller receives a credit for the Final Value Fee.

3.  When a buyer disagrees that the sale was not completed due to mutual agreement, the buyer is favored by not receiving an Unpaid Item Strike. The seller must pay the Final Value Fee. In addition, the dispute will be immediately closed after the buyer responds. The seller is not eligible to re-file an Unpaid Item Dispute.

4.  The buyer has 7 days to respond to the e-mail or pop-up message, noting the Unpaid Item Dispute. After the 7 days, the seller can close the dispute and receive a Final Value Fee Credit. The buyer then receives a strike.

### 3. The Buyer and Seller Communicate

The buyer has three options to communicate to the seller:

1.  Pay for the item to resolve the dispute. When PayPal is available, the buyer simply pays via PayPal. With other payment methods, the seller should wait until payment is received, and the check clears, before closing the dispute.

2.  Inform the seller of previous payment. Sometimes a mailed check or money order may be delayed. If payment was made, the buyer should tell the seller how, and when and where the payment was submitted. The seller then chooses the appropriate option to close the dispute.

3.  Communicate with the seller. eBay has a message area where the buyers and sellers can communicate with each other without relying on e-mail. The seller can close the dispute at any time by choosing the appropriate option.

### 4. Closing the Dispute

When the buyer responds at least once or does not respond within 7 days, the seller can close the dispute. Options include:

*   Both buyer and seller are satisfied. Here, the seller receives no Final Value Fee Credit and the buyer receives no Unpaid Item Strike.

*   Mutually agree "No Sale." The buyer does not receive an Unpaid Item Strike, the seller receives a Final Value Fee Credit, and the item is eligible for a re-list credit.

*   Seller stops communicating with the buyer. Here, the seller is credited for the Final Value Fee and the buyer receives an Unpaid Item Strike. The item can be re-listed.

Disputes can only be open for 60 days after the transaction date. Disputes that are not closed within 60 days are automatically closed. Automatic closures do not lead the seller to receive a Final Value Fee Credit and the buyer receives no Unpaid Item Strike.

> **Tip**
>
> Sellers cannot begin disputing an unpaid item if the item has already been paid for through PayPal, unless the PayPal payment was refunded.

## Con Artists

Even though eBay and government agencies have implemented programs to protect online buyers and sellers, the National Consumer League lists auction fraud as the most prevalent type of online crime. Given that fact, eBay still reports that 99.9 percent of all transactions involve honest eBay members.

To help you avoid falling into the .01 percent victim category, keep your eyes open for these fraudulent practices:

| **Bid Shilling** | |
| --- | --- |
| | Seller creates multiple user IDs to unfairly increase the number and amount of bids |
| Red Flag: | Recurring pattern of same bidders at the same seller |
| | Repeated bids by a user on multiple items of a particular seller |
| Protection: | Report such incidents with evidence to eBay through SafeHarbor and block the suspected user IDs from your listings |

| **Bid Shielding** | |
| --- | --- |
| | Multiple bidders team up to inflate the bid value to intimidate other bidders—the higher bidders retract their bids, so that the lower bidder wins the item—the seller is cheated out of making the sale at a higher price |
| Red Flag: | Bidders who continually retract their bid at the end of the auction; reoccurring groups of user IDs that show up on multiple items |
| Protection: | Same as above |

## Dishonest Descriptions

|  | Seller inflates the products features, distorts photos or hides flaws to command a higher price |
|---|---|
| Red Flag: | If something is too good to be true, there is probably a reason |
|  | Vague description |
|  | Touched-up photos |
| Protection: | Same as above |

## Final Price Changes

|  | Seller asks the buyer to pay for the exact bid for a Dutch Auction purchase rather than the lowest winning bid amount—this scam can also include surprise additional charges, such as handling fees |
|---|---|
| Red Flag: | Since final price changes happen at the end of an auction, it is difficult to protect yourself |
| Prevention: | You can avoid some conflict by confirming the price and shipping charges in an e-mail immediately after you win the auction—if the seller continues to insist on the higher price, refer the seller to the rules or shipping calculator, and report the incident to eBay |

## Deadbeat Sellers

|  | The buyer pays, but the merchandise never arrives |
|---|---|
| Red Flag: | These sellers are quick to request payment and often have false contact information |
|  | The same item and description may appear later or on a different auction site |
| Prevention: | Try to use a credit card, because you will be able to dispute the charges with the card issuer—avoid all future interaction with the seller |
|  | Report the incident to eBay and other agencies—this event constitutes mail fraud |

## Fakes and Knock-Offs

The seller lists a fake or imitation, such as clothes or accessories that claim to be by a particular designer

Red Flag: Claims that say the seller "thinks" or "believes" the item is authentic

No information about the origin of the item is available

Prevention: Do a little research to find out how to recognize a fake

Ask questions about the product and look for evasive or dismissive responses

## Loss or Damage Claims

Buyer claims the item never arrived or is damaged and demands a full refund

Red Flag: Claim is made weeks or months after shipping

Buyer immediately demands a refund before you have had time to investigate

Buyer offers to discard the merchandise

Prevention: Remind buyers to purchase insurance or tracking services

## Substituted Returns

Buyers return the item, but it is not the same as the one that was shipped

Red Flag: Early interest in return policy

Vagueness about reason for return

Protection: Provide good photos and descriptions to document condition of item up front

Return the item to the buyer with list of ways the items are dissimilar

Bar the buyer from your future auctions

## Bid Siphoning

Buyer receives an e-mail offering to sell the item for less elsewhere. While not fraudulent, this practice is against eBay's fair-bidding rules.

## Recourse and Protection

There are several avenues sellers and buyers can take to minimize loss due to fraud. Here is a list of several options:

- Always request as much contact information as the buyer is willing to provide. Sometimes this information can be verified through the phone company, which may help you down the road.

- Do not hesitate to contact a buyer if you have a problem.

- Contact SquareTrade, Inc., a free service that resolves disputes, when problems go unresolved beyond 14 days.

- Buyers should contact credit card issuers to recoup payment on goods not received.

- File a fraud alert after 30 days on eBay's site for help resolving the problem.

- Contact the National Fraud Information Center or the Internet Fraud Complaint.

## Closing the Sale

To facilitate a positive closing experience, follow these steps:

1. Check out the buyer. Does he/she have good history and feedback on the auction site?

2. Send your buyers an e-mail. They will already have been notified of their winning bid, but it is good "netiquette" for the seller to send a message. Confirm the price, payment method and shipping information.

3. Wait for payment. (Wait for a check to clear, a money order to be deposited or a credit card payment to go through.)

4. Ship the item promptly—and pack it carefully. Send the buyer an e-mail letting them know the package is on its way.

5. Provide feedback about the buyer. This should prompt them to write something about you. If you expect negative or not-so-positive feedback, consider waiting until you see what the buyer says about you first.

6. Pay the fees owed the auction site for your completed sale.

7. Hold the check (or funds) until you are sure that problems will not arise.

> **Tip**
>
> The faster you respond to inquiries, the more likely you are to receive good feedback, which is like gold in online auctions. You will also build your reputation as a trustworthy seller if you communicate regularly with the buyer.

> **Tip**
>
> An easy way to boost your customer service and feedback is to include a handwritten thank you note in your package. Throw in a business card, if appropriate.

### Handling Unsatisfied Customers

One important marketing advantage you can leverage is excellent customer service. On eBay, service is critical, because negative feedback can greatly influence future business. If others are helping to run your eBay business, it is critical that they also treat buyers well. To ensure happy buyers, follow these rules:

- Be courteous, professional and informed.
- Establish procedures for handling customer complaints and returns. Rehearse solutions before problems occur.
- Make yourself available to resolve the more serious conflicts.
- Provide comment cards or a suggestion box and respond quickly to concerns.
- Avoid false or misleading claims.
- Set high-quality standards for your products' performance.
- Honor all guarantees and warranties.
- Clearly state terms and conditions up front.
- Join a consumer advocacy group—this will show you are committed to serving your customers needs and establishes valuable credibility.

Above all, do not burn bridges. Even a difficult sale, when handled professionally and left with both parties satisfied, can lead to a mutually beneficial long-term relationship.

## Pack and Ship Smart

You will save time and expense by establishing an efficient packing area and purchasing packing supplies in volume. Your area should be free of foot traffic and stocked with all the packing supplies you need for a safe arrival. Make sure you have:

- a variety of strong boxes and reinforced envelopes in the sizes that fit your items;
- box filler, bubble wrap, peanuts or shredded paper;
- strong packing tape;
- shipping labels;
- forms, such as insurance tags;
- permanent markers; and
- utility knives.

If you are using UPS™, FedEx® or DHL®, you can get some of these items for free. You can purchase a variety of shipping supplies from the U.S. Postal Service® Web site at www.usps.com. You can also use eBay as a source for your packing supplies.

Keep it light. Loads of stuffing will increase your postage. Use lighter weight materials, like bubble wrap to cushion your items, but make sure it is sufficient to prevent damage. Here are some other tips:

- Put small items in larger boxes so they are not lost in the mail
- Let a professional, such as UPS, pack and ship large or valuable items
- Use stiffeners for photos, documents or flexible items
- If an item shakes in the box, you need to add more cushioning
- Do not over pack your item—the pressure could cause damage and the weight of increased packing supplies increases postage

Whatever shipper you choose, it is wise to request a receipt of confirmation to let you know when the package was delivered.

### No Sale?

If your item does not sell, try again.

- Post the auction one more time.
- If it does not sell twice, take a hard look at your price, your title and description.
- Consider making a change and posting one more time.

# Chapter 7
# Grow Your Business

Whether you are expanding your store's customer base to include eBay or making a career out of an eBay hobby, there are valuable strategies to reach your goal.

## Establish a Niche

What is your passion? Over time, you may have gained ample knowledge of a type of product. If you are a connoisseur of designer clothes, become the expert of a particular designer. If you dabble in antique books, position yourself as an antiquarian. If you are well-versed in music, consider specializing in selling rare CDs or vintage albums. You can leverage this experience by telling your customers about your expertise. Becoming an expert also gives you access to inventory sources that might otherwise be unavailable. Specializing helps you create a store that you can build a brand around.

## Develop a Business Plan

Applying business principles will help you achieve your goal of making a career as an eBay seller. This begins with a business plan. A well-researched business plan is the chief tool for organizing your ideas and communicating them to others. Even if you are only planning to operate from home without pursuing any loan or backing, your business plan will help define where your resources should be placed and help you consider possibilities to grow. The business plan is absolutely essential for three reasons:

1.  It allows you to objectively analyze your chances of success. The more you know, the better prepared you are for the future. Thoroughly analyze your plan in terms of potential customers and operating strategies and your bottom line.

2.  It offers solid objectives and strategies. An effective business plan is a dynamic pattern for success that continually evolves as your business grows, structuring decisions based upon objective standards.

3.  It helps you secure financing. You must sell your business to potential lenders, suppliers and distributors who will treat your proposal as an investment—they will look for proof of profits.

A complete business plan answers every question—who, what, where, when, why, how and how much? It is equally important to organize and condense your plan into a clear, concise and compelling presentation.

## Creating Your eBay Store

You can gain a more permanent commercial presence on the Web by creating an eBay store—and eBay makes it easy. Just go to the Site Map and click on Open Your Store Now under the eBay stores subhead. eBay Stores help career sellers maximize business. This is a powerful and easy-to-use tool that allows you to build your own brand on eBay and encourage buyers to purchase more.

There are three subscription levels that all offer:

*   a store URL
*   keyword search within your store
*   ability to quickly and easily create a customized, professional marketplace
*   advanced cross-promotion tools and merchandising
*   sales reports
*   real-time store traffic reports
*   inclusion in the eBay stores directory
*   automatic optimization for highest possible rankings on search engines

These features deliver the following benefits:

*   average increase of 25 percent more in sales (through incremental sales in the first 3 months are reported by most sellers*)
*   savings on listings fees

- longer inventory listings of 30, 60, 90 and 120 days or even indefinitely
- downloadable templates for business cards and other forms
- credibility as an online retailer
- organizes your items into 20 custom categories
- cross-promotional opportunities to lead your customers to related items
- free monthly reports that summarize activity
- a search engine that allows shoppers to search only your store
- tools that drive traffic to your store

The first 30 days of "owning" an eBay store are FREE, so you can try it with very little risk. After that, eBay offers different levels of stores.

*This figure is based on data from May 2002-Feburary 2003, normalized for site seasonality. No claim is made that your actual sales will increase by this average.

➡ **What Is Cross-Selling?**

If you are selling a DVD player, display other players in your inventory when buyers are in your store. When they bid, display accessories or items such as DVD cleaners and DVDs on the bid.

## Evaluate Sales

With eBay's Sales Reports Plus, store sellers have online access to their sales data. This report is available to all store sellers as part of their subscription and is broken down by listing format and category to include these statistics:

- sales
- ended listings
- percent of successful listings
- average sale price
- eBay and PayPal fees
- metrics by category
- metrics by format
- metrics by ending day or time
- buyer counts
- eBay fees
- requested unpaid item credits

## Choose from Three Store Level Subscriptions

| | BASIC | FEATURED | ANCHORED |
|---|---|---|---|
| Additional fully customizable pages in your Store | 5 Pages | 10 Pages | 15 Pages |
| FREE subscription to Selling Manager Pro | | ✔ | ✔ |
| Advanced Store traffic reporting (includes visitor path analysis and bid and buy-it-now tracking) | | ✔ | ✔ |
| Advanced Store sales reports (includes eBay marketplace data to benchmark your Store) | | ✔ | ✔ |
| Increase exposure on eBay | | ✔ on eBay Stores Pages | ✔ on eBay Stores Pages |
| Promotional dollars to spend on the eBay Keyword Program | | ✔ | ✔ |
| 24-hour dedicated live Customer Support | | | ✔ |
| Monthly Subscription Fee | $9.95 | $49.95 | $499.95 |

You can choose from three eBay store subscription levels.

### Basic Store

Lower volume sellers can start out with the Basic Store, which is affordable, at $9.95 per month and easy-to-use.

### Featured Store

Small-to-medium sized sellers who want to aggressively grow their online business can subscribe to become a Featured Store for $49.95 per month To upgrade, go to Manage Your Store and select Featured Subscription. A Featured Store offers:

- increased customization and brand control
- up to 10 fully customizable pages in your Store
- capable of minimizing the eBay Header on all your Store pages
- advanced business intelligence
- marketplace data and monthly sales reports
- sophisticated traffic reporting (to monitor buyers in your store)
- more exposure and branding opportunities

- priority placement in eBay's on-site promotions
- prepaid eBay keywords
- Selling Manager Pro to help organize your inventory (a $15.99 per month value)

**Anchored Store**

Higher-volume sellers who want to maximize their exposure on eBay can upgrade to an Anchored Store for $499.95 monthly. This option delivers a variety of tools and services. To learn more about this upgrade, e-mail anchorstores@ebay.com.

---

**Self-Promote**

Although eBay's services provide ways to market your items, why stop there? Promote your auctions as much as possible. The more you point people toward your auctions, the more potential bidders you will have. Here are ways that you can promote your auctions yourself:

- If you have a Web site, add links to your auctions there
- Place ads (or write articles) in collectors' publications, related newsletters, etc.
- Post notices on list serves and message boards

---

## Market Your Store and Earn eBay Referral Credits

Now that you have "hung out the shingle," you need to attract shoppers —and there is no reason to limit your marketing efforts to eBay. You can bring buyers to your store by creating links on Web pages outside of eBay—and earn credits on eBay.

When a user types your store's URL into their Web browser, eBay's system automatically detects their entry and interprets the user as coming from your off-eBay promotion, thus making you eligible for the Store Referral Credit.

When your store attracts a buyer who then purchases an item, you can earn a Store Referral Credit. To qualify for this credit:

- your promotional efforts must lead a buyer to enter your eBay store or one of your store inventory listings direct a location outside of eBay.
- the buyer's browser must accept cookies
- the buyer must purchase the item during the same Web browser session used to enter your store

- the purchased item must be in your store inventory format (your regular Auction and Fixed Price Listings cannot qualify for Store Referral Credit)

You can promote your eBay Store in printed materials, such as business cards, packing slips, or printed advertisements, and simply show your URL on your Store's main page. You can also include links to these parts of your Store to become eligible for the credit:

- the item page of one of your store inventory listings
- your "About Me" page
- a custom category within your Store
- a search results page within your Store, with your specified keywords

### Communicate with Buyers

E-mail and snail mail communications with buyers can help promote your store and earn the Store Referral Credit. You can use either your store's main URL in regular text or send e-mails in HTML format with clickable links to your Store, as you would do on a Web page.

More sophisticated tactics can call for mailing postcards to those who might be interested in your products, or leaving flyers in shops, park district facilities or other places where people may have an interest in your product.

Once you have set up your off-eBay promotions, your part is done. Now all you have to do is wait for the many visitors you have drawn to your Store to buy your Store inventory items.

## Establishing Your Business in the Community

### Choosing a Business Structure

Will your business be a sole proprietorship, partnership, corporation or limited liability company (LLC)? In applying for various permits, licenses and bank accounts, you will be asked which of these you plan on forming. Your accountant and attorney can help you decide which option is best for you.

Short-term considerations include structural regulations, filing fees and record-keeping requirements. These are the things that will affect you daily as you run your business. More importantly, consider long-term factors such as tax benefits, raising capital, transferring interests and asset protection. Although you may believe you will never fail, the fact is your company has only a 20 percent chance of surviving beyond 5 years.

### Sole Proprietorships

A sole proprietorship is the least costly way of starting a business. You can form a sole proprietorship by opening the door for business. There are the usual fees for registering your business name and for legal work in changing zoning restrictions and obtaining necessary licenses. Attorney's fees for starting your business will be less than for the other forms, because less document preparation is required.

### Partnerships

A partnership can be formed by simply making an oral agreement between two or more persons, but such informality is not recommended. Legal fees for drawing up a partnership agreement are higher than those for a sole proprietorship, but may be lower than incorporating. You would be wise, however, to consult an attorney to have a partnership agreement drawn up to help resolve future disputes.

### Corporations

A corporation is formed and authorized by law to act as a single entity, although it may be owned by one or more persons. It is legally endowed with rights and responsibilities and has a life of its own, independent of the owners and operators. It has been defined by the U.S. Supreme Court as "an artificial being, invisible, intangible and existing only in contemplation of the law." Think of it as a distinct and independent entity that exists separately from its owners.

Some mistakenly feel incorporating is reserved for giant companies employing hundreds and grossing millions. Single-person companies are eligible for, and should consider, corporate protection. Here are other benefits that incorporating can offer:

- **Transferable Interests**
  A corporation has the ability to raise capital by issuing shares of stock, whether public or private. Although the sale of public stock is highly regulated by both federal and state governments, ownership interest or shares of stock may be freely transferred to another party under the rules of the stockholder agreement.

  Once the interest is transferred, the new owner has all the rights and privileges associated with the former owner's interest. The Federal Trade Commission sets strict rules for issuing and publicly trading shares.

- **Tax Deductions**
  The IRS allows corporate owners to fully deduct certain fringe benefits, such as pensions, retirement plans and other profit-sharing plans, if properly documented.

- **Continuous Life**
  Unlike a partnership or sole proprietorship, a corporation has a life independent of its owners and may continue to exist despite the death or incapacity of any or all of its directors.

However, forming a corporation involves five major drawbacks:

1. Double taxation. A corporation generates its own profit, and is thus taxed separately from its members. Owners are also taxed on an individual basis, meaning a corporation is subject to "double taxation." (This may be avoided with a "subchapter S" corporation.)

2. Bureaucracy and governmental regulation. In order for the IRS to recognize a corporation as a separate entity, its directors must abide by strict regulations that govern corporate activity. Without well-maintained corporate records, the courts may disregard your corporate status and allow creditors to sue you personally for business debts. This is called "piercing the corporate veil," and happens more often than you think. States require you to file your Articles of Incorporation and sometimes bylaws. But to safely protect your corporate status, you must dutifully record all your meetings, resolutions and amendments. You must also inform the secretary of state of any other changes involving your directors, registered agent, location or corporate purpose.

3. Corporations are the most expensive form of business to organize.

4. Operating across state lines can be complicated. Corporations need to "qualify to do business" in states where they are not incorporated.

5. Ending the corporate existence, and in many cases changing even the structure of the organization, can be more complicated and costly than for other business entities.

Once you have incorporated, you have the option of filing taxes under IRS subchapter S. An S corporation, as this is called, has the corporate structure of a C or regular corporation, but enjoys the same "pass through" tax status as a partnership, sole proprietorship or LLC. This means the S corporation itself avoids "double taxation," paying no federal taxes. There are a few things to remember. Your salary must be included on the payroll and is subject to employment taxes. Health benefits are not fully deductible, as in a C corporation. However, an S corporation is allowed to "carry back" losses from prior years to offset current earnings.

Limited Liability Companies

To some business analysts, the LLC represents the "best of both worlds." First, it offers the pass-through tax status of a partnership. Members are taxed on an individual basis. The company itself pays no taxes (unlike a corporation). Second, members also enjoy limited liability protection. Risk is limited to their business investment. Personal assets are not subject to seizure from the company's creditors. Both advantages come with relatively few structural and paperwork requirements. An IRS ruling in 1988 granted LLCs this special pass-through tax status.

The owners are not personally liable for debts and obligations of the corporation. They can personally lose only to the extent of their investment in the corporation, with the exception that they may be personally liable for certain types of taxes, such as payroll taxes withheld from the employees' paychecks, but not paid to the Internal Revenue Service and state tax authorities. If the business fails or loses a lawsuit, the general creditors cannot attach the owners' homes, cars and other personal property.

To qualify, organizations must exhibit no more than two of the following four corporate characteristics:

1. Continuous life. Prevent your LLC from existing as "a separate entity" in two simple steps. Specify a dissolution date, typically 30 years, in your Operating Agreement. Also, include a special directive written in the document that allows your company to continue to exist without amending the Operating Agreement following any member's death, resignation, expulsion, bankruptcy or retirement.

2. Centralized management. While corporations typically appoint a board of directors as management, an LLC must vest management power in its members to maintain pass-through status. Although one-member LLCs may have difficulty obtaining partnership tax status, husband and wife are recognized as separate members.

3. Limited liability. A central reason for forming an LLC.

4. Free transferability of interests. Members may assign or transfer interests to a third party or creditor who is entitled to receive dividends but not allowed to vote without membership consent.

Most states require LLCs to register their Articles of Organization (similar to corporate Articles of Incorporation), the Operating Agreement (similar to corporate bylaws or a partnership agreement) and pay a fee. Check with your secretary of state for statutes that may apply to you. The disadvantages of operating as an LLC include the lack of widespread familiarity and thus, acceptance of this type of organization.

IRS rules governing insolvency may create problems for LLC owners. LLCs do not enjoy the advantages of IRS rulings when there is a sale of worthless stock or stock is sold at a loss. The sale of 50 percent or more of the ownership of the LLC in any 12-month period ends any tax advantage the company may have had with the IRS. Also, LLCs may not engage in tax-free reorganizations.

You can easily obtain the proper forms from your state's Department of Incorporation, and fill them out and file them with the secretary of state on your own. Given the proper forms, you can easily form your own corporation, S corporation, LLC or limited partnership, each offering distinct benefits.

There are other business models, such as hybrid organizations or virtual businesses, which offer other options. An example of a hybrid company is a Limited Liability Partnership. For an eBay business, this might be appropriate if you acquire some of your merchandise through your partner who lives in Japan and fulfills winning bids from his home after you forward the order. A virtual business means that you and your staff may operate from different locations using the Internet, fax machines and phones to conduct operations.

Whatever structure you choose when establishing your business, meet with an accountant and an attorney to be sure you are addressing all legal and financial obligations.

You can operate your business as a sole proprietorship, corporation or LLC under your own name, so there is no need to file an Assumed Name Affidavit.

| Business Model | Advantages | Disadvantages |
|---|---|---|
| Sole Proprietorship: A business with one owner who operates the business using his/her own name and whose income, expenses and profit are those of the owner alone. | • Easiest to get started<br>• Greatest freedom of action<br>• Maximum authority<br>• Income tax advantages in very small firms<br>• Social Security advantage to owner | • Unlimited liability<br>• Death or illness endangers business<br>• Growth limited to personal energies<br>• Personal affairs easily mixed with business |
| Partnership: A defined or implied relationship where both partners become the employee of the partnership/ business. | • Two heads better than one<br>• Additional sources of venture capital<br>• Better credit rating than corporation of similar size | • Death, withdrawal, or bankruptcy of one partner endangers business<br>• Difficult to get rid of bad partner<br>• Hazy line of authority |
| Corporation: Also called a C corporation, it is the most common corporate structure. Corporations are separate legal entities that are owned by shareholders and limited liability to shareholders so they are not personally liable for debts and obligations of the company. | • Limits liability, so personal assets are protected from creditors<br>• Able to raise capital by selling stock (requires legal help to write disclosure statement) | • Double taxation bureaucracy and governmental regulation<br>• You must also inform the secretary of state of any other changes involving your directors, registered agent, location or corporate purpose<br>• Most expensive form of business to organize<br>• Operating across state lines can be complex<br>• Ending the corporation or changing the structure can be complicated and costly |
| Limited Liability Company (LLC): A distinct business entity that offers an alternative to partnerships and corporations by combining the corporate advantage of limited liability protection with "pass-through" taxation (loses and gains) to the members, who then pay taxes or have a reduction on their personal tax return. | • Offers protection from personal liability<br>• Can help avoid self-employment tax<br>• Accommodates multiple owners or members<br>• Managing member of an LLC can deduct 100 percent of health insurance premiums | • Managing member's share of the bottom-line profit of the LLC is considered earned income, and therefore is subject to self-employment tax<br>• Members are not allowed to pay themselves "wages" |

### Registering Your Business' Name

Unless you are using your full name and operating as a sole proprietorship or general partnership, you must fill out a DBA (Doing Business As) form with the state in which you will be operating.

"Doing business as" tells the public your company's name. Naming your business is accomplished by filing a document called an Assumed Name Affidavit. This name is the one that will appear in the phone book and on your company checks and possibly your eBay ID. Called a Fictitious Name in some states, this document is filed along with your corporation, limited partnership or LLC forms and reserves your name in that state. This means filing a standard affidavit form with your county, having it notarized and publishing the affidavit several times in your local newspaper.

Your business' name is a company asset. To maximize its value, the ideal name should:

- describe your business but not limit it to specifics
- be easy to say, spell and remember—simplicity sells
- fit the character and clientele of your enterprise
- be composed of an acronym if you plan to use several words
- if you will also depend on business from the Yellow Pages, start with a letter early in the alphabet—customers with no preference start with "A" and work their way toward "Z" when researching sellers
- never start with an article—do not risk being listed under "A" or "The"
- be clever but not corny or deliberately misspelled
- make sure the name is unique. Look in phone books to see if the name has been taken. Check the Federal Trademark Registry as well as state registries to make sure no other company has exclusive federal or state trademark rights to the name. You can even do a preliminary free search on the Internet. Attorneys generally charge between $50 and $500 to do such a search. If the name you use is deceptively similar to a trademarked name or one already in use, you may be forced to give up the name or face a lawsuit.

The advantage of establishing your business with a name is that your business becomes official and legal. It can help you borrow money, sell your business and open bank accounts. However, your city may ask you to get a business license and pay a city tax. You will also be asked to comply with city inspectors and other regulators. If you move to another county or change your name, you will need to re-file.

## Build Your Brand

You can take your business to another level that will help increase awareness and help you be more memorable, by building your brand. Like a big corporation, you would have exclusive right to use your business' name.

## Trademark Your Name

When you established your business, you may have created a name separate from your own. To build a brand, separate from your own name, you could consider trademarking your business' name, graphic or tagline.

The first step is investigating whether anyone already has a trademark on your name. You can do a trademark search by visiting www.uspto.gov. If you are free to use your chosen name, graphic or tagline, you need to file a trademark application with the U.S. Patent and Trademark Office, which will cost several hundred dollars.

A trademark is a long-term investment that you can use to leverage recognition and awareness among your customers. It is the first step in building a brand that you can use to market your products. After all, eBay has built a brand that is easily recognized and trusted by millions of shoppers. There is no reason why you cannot eventually do the same.

## Develop Your Logo

Start with a logo. You want to turn your business' name into a graphic that can be used consistently in order to build recognition. Unless you have a professional graphic designer who can help you, keep it simple. Your logo can be a particular font with a unique treatment. Choose a style that is consistent with your products. In other words, if you are going to specialize in selling rock music, you do not want your name to look like it belongs on a baby product. Also, design your name in black and white, because it will be printed in black and white most often and you need to be sure it will work without color. Another factor is the name or logo's ability to be reduced. If you make your name smaller to appear on a business card, make sure you can still read it.

The secret to building your brand is consistency. Do not let the way your logo appears vary in any way—whether on a Web site, ad, business card or letterhead.

**Keys to an Effective Trademark:**
- memorable
- appropriate
- recognizable
- used consistently
- easy to read

## Sales Tax License

Most states require businesses to charge a sales tax for goods sold to customers in the state. To collect and deposit these funds with the state requires a sales tax license. This license is also known as a resale license, reseller's or seller's permit or sales tax certificate.

The license has benefits. You can purchase goods at wholesale prices without paying a sales tax, which will help you become more profitable. It also defines your business as a retail establishment, which gives you credibility. Wholesalers may require an Employer Identification Number (EIN) if you are a partnership or a corporation, or your Social Security number if you are a sole proprietor.

The law requires that you charge your customers the sales tax and regularly deposit the funds with the state. Be sure to file and pay your periodic sales tax deposits on time. Once you fall behind, it is difficult to catch up. Charging sales tax only applies to sales to in-state customers.

**Sales Tax-Free States**
Alaska
Delaware
Montana
New Hampshire
Oregon

### Business License

Most municipalities require you to have a business license, even if you operate from your home. When you file an Assumed Name Affidavit, which you may do when opening a business bank account, local authorities may be alerted to the fact that you are in operation. The business license establishes you as a legitimate business.

### Tax Number

When establishing your business, you need a tax number to file tax returns. Sole proprietors use their Social Security number on tax returns, because the business is not a separate taxable entity. Partnerships, corporations and LLCs require a federal EIN. Also, an estimated tax must be paid on a quarterly basis.

### Business Bank Account

Unless your business is a sole proprietorship, your business should have a bank account that is separate from your personal bank account. To open this account, the bank will ask for an Assumed Name Affidavit.

### Insurance

By purchasing insurance for your small business, you protect your business' assets and, unless you have established a corporation, you protect your own. You should have business coverage for your inventory if you are stocking significant items. Talk to your insurance agent about your individual situation.

**Tax Bulletin**

Since you will be self-employed, no one is taking taxes out of your paycheck. That means you will need to make quarterly payments to the IRS and your state. Not making these payments can result in expensive penalties, so be sure to talk with your accountant to determine how much should be paid and how to adjust your payments as you grow your business.

## Hiring Employees or Independent Contractors

With great products that are presented well, and a successful marketing plan implemented, you could become really busy. This is the time to realize that you could make more money, if you had help. Additional people can be valuable in assisting with:

- fulfillment
- bookkeeping
- data entry
- photography
- creating auction ads
- auction management
- customer follow-up
- customer service
- Web development

It is important to recognize the legal difference in hiring an employee or an independent contractor. When starting out or operating a small company and in need of help, an independent contractor is usually a simpler, better option, because there are less laws that affect your relationship. Here are a few conditions that define an employee:

- receives benefits
- receives on-the-job training
- employer supplies tools
- works on a set schedule
- requires instruction to perform job
- may supervise other workers
- may quit at any time
- works exclusively for one source

|  | Advantages | Disadvantages |
|---|---|---|
| Employee | • More control over time, performance and continuity | • Must provide minimum benefits |
|  |  | • Must withhold taxes |
|  |  | • Must pay workman's compensation insurance |
|  |  | • Subject to employment laws regarding overtime pay, etc. |
| Independent Contractor | • No need to comply with most laws concerning employment | • May require higher hourly pay, which can be offset by above employee costs |
|  | • Offers flexibility |  |

If you do hire an independent contractor, be sure to draw up an agreement that specifies your relationship, fee, expectations/specifications, deliverables and deadlines. If your contractor fails to do the job, you can claim damages. On the other hand, when an employee is disappointed he/she can quit at any time and you cannot make any claim.

## Learn More and Stay Current

Managing a successful business means dedicating some time to learning as much as you can about the products you sell, new business strategies, and eBay's latest buying and seller programs and policies. In fact, eBay offers ample learning opportunities for beginners as well as seasoned users through eBay University. There are also seminars in cities across the country where you can learn the latest tips on successful online selling. Here is a summary of highlights from eBay's courses:

### Selling Basics

This class is a good place to start to learn the basics. You will learn how to:

- open a seller account
- research and create listings
- improve descriptions and photos
- smart pricing
- open and use a PayPal account
- monitor your listings
- complete transactions

### Beyond the Basics

If you have been selling on eBay occasionally, and want to learn how to get the most out of your listings, this class offers the more advanced information you need. You will learn how to:

- start and/or grow an eBay business
- choose the right listing format
- create compelling listings
- use eBay listing tools
- market your eBay business
- manage your listings
- pack and ship inventory
- use online PayPal payments

### eBay for Business

If you are running an eBay business, or plan to, you will learn many of the important things you need to know about operating your business day-to-day —and grow it. Created and presented by experts in their fields, in association with Entrepreneur Magazine, this class teaches attendees how to:

• handle business tax issues
• maintain income and balance sheets
• choose a business lawyer or accountant
• manage operations and inventory
• hire employees
• leverage trends that will impact eBay sales
• find new sources of inventory

Another source of knowledge is eBay Live!, the annual eBay conference held each year in June. Check the eBay site map for the conference announcement. Local business associations also hold many events that can offer information on business management. In addition, professional associations, such as the American Management Association, hold business seminars that help entrepreneurs.

## Go International

There is no reason to think small. Buyers around the world are looking for American goods and you can help supply them through eBay sales in more than 25 countries. Aside from export policies, there are four areas that need to be considered when dealing with buyers around the globe: language and communication, shipping, payment and fraud.

### Language and Communication

You may be surprised at how many people in foreign countries speak English. However, there are Web sites that translate a multitude of languages if you do not understand an e-mail. You should also check out international telephone rates, so that you can speak to customers on the phone.

### Shipping

Although sending merchandise to a foreign country is fairly easy, the costs to ship can dramatically increase. Most shippers, including the U.S. Postal Service®, DHL®, FedEx® and UPS™, send packages internationally. Make sure your foreign customers understand the amount of your shipping charges.

## Payment

The biggest challenge in handling international sales is ensuring prompt, accurate payment. However, with PayPal now serving in more than 35 countries, it is getting easier. You just have to make sure the money is converted into U.S. dollars or you will only be able to use your payment in the country of origin. Western Union® is another tried-and-true service for sending payment. If you accept checks, or even money orders, make sure they clear before shipping the item. Counterfeit documents are not unusual.

## Fraud

Between hackers and credit card thieves, fraud abounds. Be careful and use the most secure payment method available. If you are a victim of fraud, there is little recourse when selling internationally.

International selling is also a good way to connect with others in foreign markets who have access to goods you can buy to sell. Create an alliance and increase your volume. Meanwhile, read up on export/import policies and customs practices to keep the sales moving smoothly.

# Appendix 1
# Resources

## General Information

SAMS Teach Yourself e-Auctions—Today: Bidding, Buying and Selling at eBay and Other Online Auction Sites by Preston Gralla, (1999)

Kovel's Bid, Buy, and Sell Online by Ralph M. Kovel and Terry Kovel, (2001)

eBay Business the Smart Way: Maximize Your Profits on the Web's #1 Auction Site by Joseph T. Sinclair, (2004)

How to Sell Anything on eBay...and Make a Fortune by Dennis L. Prince, (2003)

The Unofficial Guide to eBay and Online Auctions by Dawn E. Reno, Bobby Reno and Mark Butler (Editor), (2000)

Pros and Cons of the LLC Model by David Meier, (2003)

Direct Mail Copy That Sells! by Herschell Gordon Lewis, (1984)

## Small Business Resources

| | |
|---|---|
| American Management Association© | www.amanet.org/seminars/index.htm |
| American Small Business Association (ASBA) | www.asbaonline.com |
| BusinessLaw.gov | www.businesslaw.gov |
| Entrepreneur.com® | www.entrepreneur.com |
| SCORE (a resource partner with the U.S Small Business Administration) | www.score.org |
| U. S. Small Business Administration | www.sba.gov |

## Shipping Resources

| | |
|---|---|
| DHL® | www.dhl.com |
| FedEx® | www.fedex.com |
| Stamps.com™ | www.stamps.com |
| United Parcel Service™ | www.ups.com |
| United States Postal Service® | www.usps.com |
| International Mail Calculator | http://ircalc.usps.gov |

## Legal Resources

| | |
|---|---|
| Occupational Safety & Health Administration | www.osha.gov/dcsp/smallbusiness/index.html |

## Fraud

| | |
|---|---|
| Federal Trade Commission (FTC) | www.ftc.gov |
| | 1.877.FTC.HELP (382.4357) |
| | TDD/TTY 1.866.653.4261. |

## Tax and Financial Information

| | |
|---|---|
| Quicken | www.quicken.com |
| Internal Revenue Service | www.irs.gov/businesses/small |
| GE Capital | www.ge.com/capital/smallbiz/ |

## Purchasing Inventory

| | |
|---|---|
| 99centwholesale.com | www.99centwholesale.com |
| Global Sources (Product and trade information for volume buyers) | www.globalsources.com |

## Creating Listings

| | |
|---|---|
| Getting Started with HTML | www.w3.org/MarkUp/Guide |
| HTML Goodies | www.htmlgoodies.com/primers/basics.html |

## Language Translators

| | |
|---|---|
| AltaVista | http://babel.altavista.com |
| Free-Translator.com | www.free-translator.com |

## Other Auction Sites

| | |
|---|---|
| Amazon.com® Auctions | http://auctions.amazon.com |
| AuctionDiner.com,Inc. | www.bidway.com |
| The Auction Guild | www.theauctionguild.com |
| Auction Patrol | www.auctionpatrol.com |
| Auction Saloon | www.auctionsaloon.com |
| AuctionAddict.com | www.auctionaddict.net |
| Auctiva Auction Glossary | www.auctiva.com/help/glossary.asp |
| Bidville, Inc. | www.bidville.com |
| eBay Learning Center | www.ebay.com/education |
| The Internet Auction List | www.internetauctionlist.com |
| National Auctioneers Association | www.auctioneers.org |
| National Mail Order Association | www.nmoa.org |
| Popula Company, Inc. | www.popula.com/categories/current |
| Pottery Auction™ | www.potteryauction.com |
| QuicklySell Auctions | www.quicklysell.com |
| Romahawk Auctions | www.romahawk.com |
| SellYourItem.com | www.sellyouritem.com |
| uBid | www.ubid.com |
| Vendio (formerly AuctionWatch) | www.vendio.com |
| qxl.com (European) | www.qxl.com |
| Yahoo!® Auctions | http://auctions.shopping.yahoo.com |

## Publications

How to Do Everything with Your eBay Business (McGraw-Hill) by Greg Holden, (2003)

Everyday Law (Socrates Media)

Everyday Legal Forms & Agreements (Socrates Media)

The New York Times, "EBay Merchants Trust their Eyes, and the Bubble Wrap" by Kate Murphy, October 24, 2004.

# Appendix 2
# Forms/Tools Included on CD

Ad Listing Checklist and Worksheet

Balance Sheet

Buyer Evaluation Report

eBay Monthly Expense Report

Feedback Follow-up Log

Gross Profit Margin Worksheet

Inventory Record

Marketing Checklist

Monthly Income Report

Sales Income Report

Time Log